FAMILIES AROUND THE WORLD

A family from
IRAQ

John King

WAYLAND

FAMILIES AROUND THE WORLD

> **Abed Ali and his family are members of Saddam Hussein's Baath Party. The Saleh-Ali family was chosen to be in this book by the Iraqi government.**

Cover: The Saleh-Ali family outside their home with all their possessions.
Title page: Abed and Alia with their five children.
Contents page: The memorial to Iraqi people who died in the wars between Iraq and Iran, and in the Gulf War.

Series editor: Katie Orchard
Series designer: Tim Mayer
Book designer: Jean Wheeler
Production controller: Carol Titchener

Picture Acknowledgements: All the photographs in this book were taken by Alexandra Boulat. The photographs were supplied by Material World/Impact Photos and were first published by Sierra Club Books in 1994 © Copyright Alexandra Boulat/Material World. The map artwork on page 4 is produced by Peter Bull.

First published in 1997 by Wayland Publishers Limited
61 Western Road, Hove
East Sussex, BN3 1JD, England

© Copyright 1997 Wayland Publishers Limited

Find Wayland on the internet at http://www.wayland.co.uk

Typeset by Jean Wheeler
Printed and bound by G. Canale & C.S.p.A., Italy

British Library Cataloguing in Publication Data
King, John
  A family from Iraq. – (Families around the world)
  1. Family – Iraq – Juvenile literature
  2. Iraq – Social life and customs – Juvenile literature
  I. Title
  306.8'5'09567

ISBN 0 7502 2008 2

Contents

Introduction

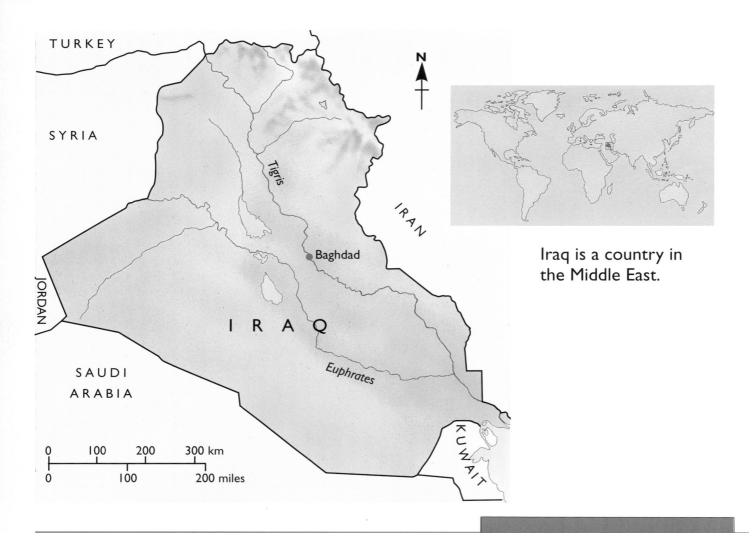

Iraq is a country in the Middle East.

REPUBLIC OF IRAQ

Capital city:	Baghdad
Size:	438,320 square kilometres
Number of people:	19,500,000
Main language:	Arabic
People:	Arab 79%, Kurdish 16%, Turkish 2%, Persian 3%.
Religion:	Mainly Muslim
Currency:	Iraqi Dinar

THE SALEH-ALI FAMILY

Size of family:	11, living in two houses
Size of homes:	Both 200 square metres
Work week:	Average: 42 hours
Most valuable possessions:	Abed: Family and television Alia: Jewellery and children Hala: Baghdad Game
Income per person:	US$1,940 each year

The Saleh-Ali family is an ordinary Iraqi family. They have put everything that they own outside their home so that this photograph could be taken.

Meet the family

Saleh household:
1 Mahdi, father, 74
2 Shaïmaa, mother, 59
3 Amira, daughter, 34
4 Falah, son, 21

Ali household:
5 Alia, Saleh family's eldest daughter, 42
6 Abed, Alia's husband, 45
7 Wasan, daughter, 19
8 Sahar, daughter, 17
9 Hala, daughter, 12
10 Ahmad, son, 7
11 Suher, daughter, 18 months

AFTER THE WAR

Iraq is ruled by President Saddam Hussein. In 1990 his army invaded Kuwait. The United Nations punished Iraq by preventing it from selling oil and buying goods from outside the country. This means that life for many of the people of Iraq has been difficult.

The Saleh-Ali family live in two houses on the outskirts of Baghdad, the capital city of Iraq. Mahdi and Shaïmaa live with two of their children, Amira and Falah, in the house shown in the picture on page 5. Their eldest daughter, Alia, lives with her husband, Abed, and their five children in another house nearby.

'It's fun having a large family. There is always someone to play with.' *Hala.*

A home in Iraq

Baghdad is very hot in the summer. Roof terraces can be cool places to sit in the evenings.

A FULL HOUSE

Iraqi families often have many children. Grown-up sons and daughters sometimes live very near their parents, or share a house with them.

The family's houses are built of brick, covered with cement. The Saleh-Ali family owns both of their houses. Shaïmaa and Mahdi bought their house thirteen years ago. Abed and Alia live in the house where Abed was born. Abed's house has been in his family for two generations.

A Room for Everything

There are six rooms in both houses. Each house has a special living room with chairs, a table and sofas where visitors sit on special occasions. There is also a living room for everyday use, and each house has a kitchen. The bedrooms are upstairs, and the living rooms and the kitchen are on the ground floor.

Hala always sits at the small table in the living room to do her homework.

'I love my clothes and I like to be able to look smart if I go out in the evening.' *Amira.*

Amira has her own bedroom. She likes to keep it private and locks the door every day.

Decorations

Inside each house, the walls are painted in white or plain colours. In the rooms, there are some pictures of places in Iraq and pictures of President Saddam Hussein. The furniture is very plain.

In the kitchen there is a cooker that runs on bottled gas. Each kitchen also has a freezer and a refrigerator.

'I love to be in my kitchen, where everything is exactly how I want it to be.' *Shaïmaa.*

Food and cooking

Shaïmaa loves to cook for her family.

KUBBA

Kubba is a typical Iraqi dish. Shells made of a mixture of wheat and minced meat are filled with more meat, onions, spices and nuts. The *kubba* are then fried and served with vegetables or yoghurt. They take a long time to make but they are very good to eat!

A meal made by Shaïmaa for her family usually includes vegetables, potatoes, salad, lemons and bread. The family usually eats meals that they make at home, although kebabs and other food can be bought at shops and restaurants.

Tasty Kebabs

Since the Gulf War, there have been shortages of some food. Now the family only eats meat twice a week, usually served as kebabs, or *kubba*.

In her house, Shaïmaa usually sits on the floor to cook in the old-fashioned way. Her daughter, Alia, stands up to cook.

Shopping

The family spends a lot of money on food. Prices are high and often go up, although the government tries to keep them down. It is traditional in Iraq for men to buy the food. Mahdi has always been proud of his ability to buy good vegetables or a tasty piece of meat. But this tradition is changing. Mahdi's daughters, Alia and Amira, like to go to the shops and choose the food themselves.

Street vendors such as this one in the centre of Baghdad offer food for sale to passers by.

A Good Breakfast

For breakfast, the family always has tea and milk, with cheese, bread, eggs and potatoes. When Hala and Ahmad come home from school, they are hungry and usually have a snack. A typical midday meal for the children is vegetables, eggs and sometimes cooked chicken, rolled up in a pancake.

Shaïmaa always makes a tasty yoghurt drink to go with spicy food.

Eating Together

The Saleh-Ali family eats together on Friday evenings, on festival days, and whenever there is a special reason to celebrate. The whole family likes being together because it is a good time to share family news.

'The family loves my cooking. Everyone says that they would rather eat at home than at a restaurant.' *Shaïmaa.*

Food is an important part of family life in Iraq, just as it is in other Arab countries. The family likes to eat at home, but sometimes they enjoy food from a restaurant for a change. Iraqi families spend a lot of time together, and big family meals are special occasions.

Everyone sits round a mat on the floor of the living room to eat.

Working hard

When Mahdi was younger, he worked in the oil industry.

WOMEN AT WORK

Iraq is different from some other Arab countries, where women are not allowed to have jobs. Many women work in Iraq. The jobs that women do are very important for the country and for the incomes of Iraqi families.

The Oil Industry

Mahdi is seventy-four years old and has retired. He spent most of his working life building oil pipelines. Mahdi also worked abroad in Libya and in Sri Lanka.

'There are no new cars in Iraq, but I look after this one well. It gets me to the office, and the whole family likes to go out for drives in it at the weekend.' *Abed*.

Keeping Busy

Abed is ready to set off for work in his car.

Abed has a job in an office, where he is a civilian worker for the Iraqi army. During the week, Abed drives Alia to work on his way to his office. Alia works as a teacher at a primary school.

When the work at the office or the shop is over, there is still the washing-up to be done!

Wasan and her aunt Amira both work in a shop at Baghdad Airport. They work there every day except Friday, from eight o'clock in the morning until three o'clock in the afternoon. It's quite hard work, especially when there are a lot of customers. At the end of the day, Wasan and Amira are usually very tired from having to spend most of the day on their feet.

Falah works hard as a student. He is learning to be a musician at the Baghdad Academy of Music. Falah would like to earn his living playing with a band and making records. The instrument he plays is called an *oudh*. It is a traditional instrument in Arab countries and is shaped a little like a guitar. Classical and popular music can be played on it. A good *oudh* is expensive, so Falah takes good care of his.

Falah plays a melody on his *oudh* for his friends.

School and play

Hala (in the middle of the group) is at the top of her class in school.

Studying Hard

Hala and Ahmad work hard at school. They both hope to get good jobs one day. The local school is open from seven o'clock in the morning until three o'clock in the afternoon. But Hala and Ahmad spend only three hours there each day. There aren't enough teachers for them to spend the whole day there.

RELIGION AT SCHOOL

In Iraq, most people are Muslims. Studying religion is a very important part of the school day. The children begin to learn about Islam when they are very young.

Playtime

After school, Ahmad loves to play football with his friends. His favourite toy is his plastic football. But he also plays with his baby sister, Suher.

'When I study the Qu'ran, our holy book, I wear gloves to keep the pages clean.' *Ahmad.*

Spare time

The whole family enjoys watching television in their spare time. Ahmad likes the football programmes best.

Most families in Iraq like to visit friends and talk during their spare time. Men like to sit in cafés, where they play games, such as dominoes, and drink tea.

Watching television

The family spends a lot of time together. In the evenings they like to watch television. There is a programme with Arabic pop music each evening that Wasan and Sahar love to watch. At nine o'clock each evening Abed likes to watch the news.

Holidays

During holidays, the Saleh-Ali family sometimes visits a little country house that it owns outside Baghdad. Hala and Ahmad enjoy sleeping in strange beds and playing in a different garden. The family can't go further away at the moment because it would be too expensive.

Abed and Ahmad often watch television together.

'I wear a shirt and trousers to go to the office, but during my spare time I like to wear traditional Iraqi clothes.' *Abed*.

The family often enjoys a stroll down their street.

A TIME TO PRAY

Religion is very important in Iraq. On Fridays the men go to the mosque to pray, but the women usually pray at home.

Often the family visits a special place, such as a historic mosque. They sometimes go out into the countryside in the car and then go for a walk or have a picnic. Sometimes Abed goes to a café to meet his friends and play backgammon.

Religion

The Saleh-Ali family is Muslim. They have texts from the Qu'ran on the walls. Shaïmaa is the only member of the family who wears the traditional Islamic scarf to cover her head.

'I pray in the living room of my house, five times a day.' *Shaïmaa.*

The future

The Saleh-Ali family all hope for a better future. Falah wants to succeed with his music. Hala is doing well at school, and her parents hope she will have a good career. Ahmad would like to be a footballer and play for Iraq.

A BETTER FUTURE

Many thousands of Iraqi men and women have died in wars since 1980. The Gulf War is still fresh in many people's minds. Most Iraqis hope that their country can look forward to peace.

'One day everything will be different. I hope there will be a better future for my children.' *Abed.*

28

Shaïmaa wants everything to be the same as it was before the wars.

Timeline

749	Beginning of Muslim rule in Baghdad.
1258	Fall of Baghdad to Mongol invaders from Central Asia.
1534	The Ottoman (Turkish) Empire captures Iraq.
1918	Ottoman Empire defeated in the First World War.
1932	Iraq joins the League of Nations and becomes independent.
1958	Iraq becomes a republic.
1979	Saddam Hussein takes power in Iraq.
1980	Iraq invades Iran.
1990	Iraq invades Kuwait. The Gulf War begins. United Nations forces a trade ban on Iraq.
1991	Iraq surrenders to the Allied Forces.
1996	The United Nations allows Iraq to export some oil.

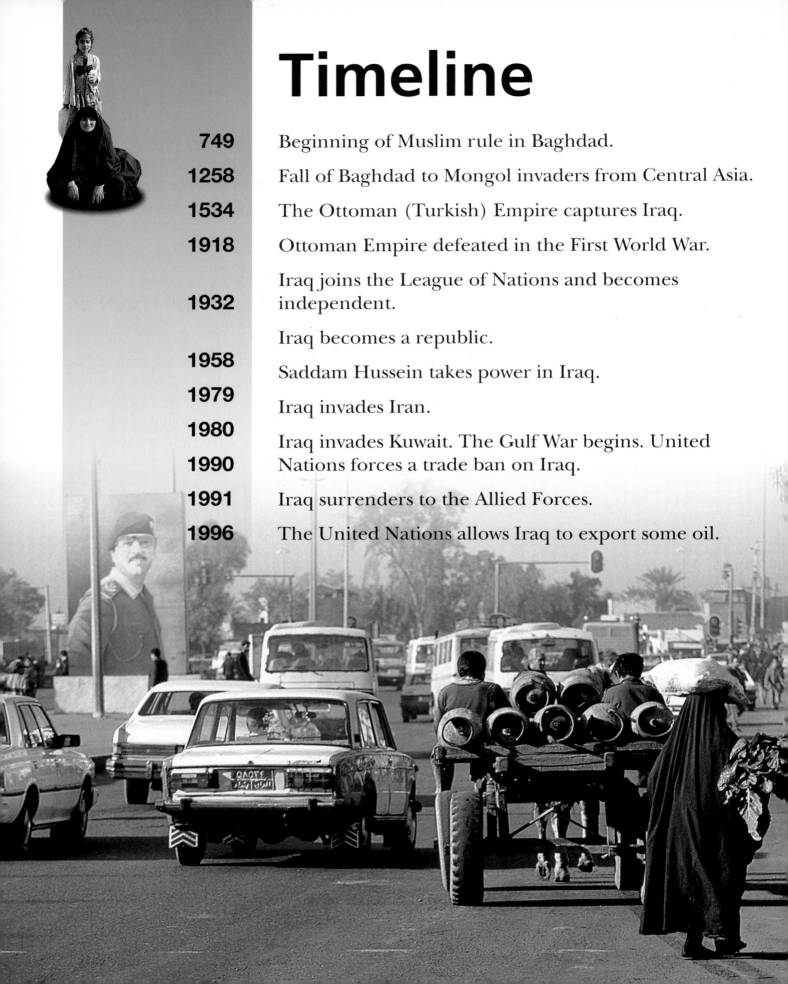

Glossary

Academy A school for students, especially of music or art.

Civilian Someone who is not a soldier.

Independent Able to make your own choice about how to act.

Islam The religion founded by Muhammed. There are one billion Muslims in the world today.

League of Nations A society of nations set up after the First World War.

Middle East The part of the world in which Iraq is situated. Other Middle Eastern countries include Egypt and Israel.

Mosque A building where Muslims gather together to pray.

Muslim A follower of the religion of Islam.

Republic A government in which all the members are elected.

United Nations (UN) A group made up of countries around the world, which works to bring peace and a better life for everyone.

Further information

Books to read:

Books for younger readers about Iraq are difficult to find. Older readers might like to read *Conflict in the Middle East* by John King (Wayland, 1994).

Organizations:

The following organizations have a selection of information and resources about everyday life in the Arab world:

Council for Arab–British Understanding, 21 Collingham Road, London SW5 8NU.

Museum of Mankind, 6 Burlington Gardens, London W1.

Index